Becoming Vulnerable

JOSHUA CORWIN

Dear Kelly,

Please be vulnerable throughout life's margins!

Love,

—Josh

P.S. Thanks for being my first babysitter.

Published by Baxter Daniels Ink Press/International Word Bank
1055 Lincoln Boulevard, Santa Monica, CA 90403

Baxter Daniels Ink Press/International Word Bank books and products are available in bookstores. Baxter Daniels Ink Press/International Word Bank also publishes its books in a variety of electronic formats. Some content that appears in print may not be available in electronic books.

ISBN: 978-0-9963927-7-8

Library of Congress Control Number: 2020904910

Printed in the United States of America
FIRST EDITION
1st Impression

Copyright © 2020 Joshua Corwin

All rights reserved.

ISBN: 978-0-9963927-7-8

Library of Congress Control Number: 2020904910

"A beautiful, powerful journey mapping a very human soul."

Ellyn Maybe, author of *The Cowardice of Amnesia* and *Walking Barefoot in the Glassblowers Museum*

"Joshua Corwin provides readers with an honest and open portrayal of the addictions and disorders that have challenged him since youth. [...] Corwin journeys through years of emotionally and physically crippling nadirs to reach a life now filled with grace and gratitude, ever mindful of the events that have helped shape him into the person he is today."

Rich Ferguson, author of *New Jersey Me* and *8th & Agony*

"This poetry takes my breath away. Cuts like a knife. Opens wounds and heals them. The words of Joshua Corwin, so precisely chosen, are rhythmical, powerful, and evocative. I read his work again and again and each time I discover new layers of wisdom and hope."

Barbara Straus Lodge, Essayist, Founder of Above The Noise Foundation

"Joshua Corwin's Becoming Vulnerable *is a remarkable window into the poetic mind in tense, exaltive and poignant conversation with itself. At times peering through the tangle of his own writing, at other times displaying a dawning gratitude for all the miles that he's come and a newfound knowledge that he has the strength to keep going (and keep writing it all into life), these poems are spare and haunting, lyrical and diagnostic. Not to be missed."*

David Rocklin, author of *The Luminist* and *The Night Language*

BECOMING VULNERABLE

Table of Contents

FOREWORD

These lyrics cry out from the heart. They are confessional in the deep sense, conveying, beyond the feelings and emotions we have expected from songs played on the lyre since Ancient Greece and Rome, the deep anguish of past addictions, beyond drugs, to a warped sense of the self, extravagant overrating's that like other addictions have been overcome, in part thanks to the confessional of and on the page, confessing to itself no less than those who read the page.

"Memory Smile," for example, appropriately happens in a Starbucks, that special place that replicates itself in untold reflections around neighborhoods and the world. The poem too centers on reflections, what is thought and felt no less than what is seen. It is not a relation of something that transpired; it is happening as the reader reads. The "I" sees someone like himself through the glass. How like? Exactly like. It is his reflection in the glass, cast back to him from the glass, and causes him to reflect on what he was and is, to confess that to himself as well as you and me, who have opened this page, and are moved now to reflect both on him and ourselves.

Such is the case, too, in celebrating ones limitations through morning rituals in "Gratitude After Breakfast" or recognizing during a telephone conversation the unique virtue of one who taught him the most virtuous form of charity proposed by Moses Maimonides, giving anonymously. At "12:01 AM," he "can hear the shine in your eyes." In "The Update," just the phrase, "a pacifist in rage," opens doors of deep understanding.

Enjoy these poems. They will open your eyes too to sounding depths in this special world.

ALBERT WACHTEL, *Pitzer College*
Professor of Creative Studies

CLAREMONT, 2019.

INTRODUCTION

I have been in therapy since I was five years old. I have been sober for the last four years. I am 26 years old as I write this now. And my entire life's modus operandi has been about perseverance. I was the kid who needed a therapist or a counselor at every play date. My parents didn't think I would have a bar mitzvah or go to college. I didn't have friends over in high school or even have a single play date in middle school. I did have a bar mitzvah, and I went to Pitzer College in Claremont, CA, where I received a B.A. in mathematics and a minor in philosophy. I was the addict who smoked weed for two nights in a row like a crack head and thought nobody understood me and nobody could understand me because I was different. I was unique. I had friends but it was all centered around drugs and alcohol. My life was a ball of fear trying to break free and hoping to get others to like me.

When I got sober, I took time off from college. After a year of sobriety, I had an out-of-body experience meditating in a shrine. When I returned to college and used my experience to fuel my studies, I started from the ground up in philosophy and cognitive neuroscience, and wrote a thesis on "Executive Qualia and their Relation to Mystical Experience."
Now, with this book, I utilize my experience as an individual with autism and as an addict who is sober and in recovery, to give back to the world with this collection of poetry, to become vulnerable.

I thought vulnerability was a weakness. But in truth it is a strength. The truth is I might be different and unique in my own special way, as is everyone, but there are others like me. And I hope they are reading these words, and I ask them to please be vulnerable within the margins.

JOSHUA CORWIN
LOS ANGELES, 2020.

For my grandpa, Mert.

Your last words to me,

"Don't ever stop writing."

GRANDPA

THE PASSAGE

My hand   feels

Your   heartbeat

You can't   smile

Blood   echoes

Esophagus'   quiver

Pouring

     Down

        Your

           Lips

How do I say goodbye?

Hands—
Smile in squeeze

Grab love
By the forehead,
Kiss

Some can't handle
The silence

They aren't comfortable
With the passage

LITTLE ENSŌS

For my grandpa, Mert.
Your last words to me,
"Don't ever stop writing."

I can't stop to feel this moment.

It's too painful

to listen to the words engulf
my otherworldly head.

It creates a space for death.

Reminds me of the emptiness inside.

Why do I feel so alien?
So foreign, so strange?

I can't shape this feeling.
I can't mold this...

I can't stop washing dishes.

If I turn off the faucet,
the flow might stop.

If I move on,
I might forget you.

I don't want to cry you away
and cry myself into isolation.

I don't want to stop washing—
I won't stop washing

dishes.

Making perfect, little
ensōs on the spoon.

I can't lift
my head

up

out

of

this
sink.

I let the faucet cry for me

because I can't handle

the pain.

Photograph by Joshua Corwin. 2019.

HELLO GRANDPA

I have a special relationship with hummingbirds.
My mom told me they are the smallest birds in the world.
They represent gratitude and humility, love and godshots.
The latter needs some explaining. Let me hum:

God graced me with sobriety on August 13, 2015.
I was sitting on a park bench around the corner from my
parents' house at this place called the "view site." Over-
looking valleys, peaks, nadirs & zeniths representative of
despair & the bottomless pit: an abyssal gorge of treason
against my raison d'être. Smoking a joint & looking to the
sky. Overlooking Pacific Coast Highway. I didn't know
why I was smoking & doing what I was doing. — This
substance, no longer sustenance for me. My dog by my
internal fireside, peering deep into my inferno, blazing
like the doobie. — Dubious, I cried out. Answerless…
No response. No reason. Pain psychic & depressive.
Feeling psychotic.

At one of my first Twelve Step anonymous meetings,
a fellow in this group of brave souls banded together
to redirect the flames to burn brightly, rather than skewer wild
boars — shared about hummingbirds & godshots:
Little events. Coincidences and winks from God. Doesn't mean
anything. It's just a visible wink. Blinking in and out —Tzim-
Tzumic vessels, breaths, smiles. (I regained my faith in Judaism
through the process of the Twelve Steps, particularly with
receiving anonymous Chassidic texts, and ninth-step amends to
my childhood rabbi …)

When I was nearly two years sober, I moved into an
apartment by myself. Living on my own, the neighbor above
would shine a hummingbird feeder out my window. Balcony
greeted song & winged love.
I'd hear their wings flapping, music napping solace to
resound within, as I meditate. Once in a while, I'd sip from a
coffee mug—given by mother—a hummingbird etched, read

7

"begin each day with a grateful heart" & I'd sip,
drink in the hummingbird humming, hovering outside my
window... The neighbor, casting ballots of golden chimes.
As cars passed on Figueroa.
      We would look each other in the eyes. Angel & man.
Angelic, this winged waiter would dish out gratitude,
me sipping coffee from its etched Talmud, listen to
rabbinical analysis on YouTube; and would follow
me showering the dove into my own personal Mikvah of song.

      Sometimes, these creatures would present (and protect)
themselves to me on the grassy mounds of belonging
out in Claremont. I'd meditate, rejoice & remember;
eyes closed, open dove-songs from solace sheltered in the Lord
belonging not just to the grassy pasture-place, but also
to the winged bird inside me. Resonating raison d'être . . .

      When I taught a one-day course — a godshot
too long to express, but some bits & pieces I'll address . . .
I pulled a book out from the Honnold Mudd Library. I was bored
& exhausted, reading for philosophy of language
seminar. And I was drawn to a book. *Consciousness & Tradition.*
I took the book, read. And felt myself humming, hovering.
That feeling remembered again.
      I found it in my bag a few days later, when I
taught a course on "The Art of Story Weaving Experience." Sitting
on the patio of the inside-out classroom at Harvey Mudd; muddy
waters washed away as a hummingbird hovered above my shoulder.

      Yesterday was July 27th. I drove to the view site. The place
where I last used. To scatter there ashic, dustic, rustic remains of
my late grandpa Mert. The dishes in my soul sink. Emotionally
tone deaf in my solar plexuses & aortic authenticity. I called a friend
from the Twelve-Step meeting I first attended. I was humming soon.
      Five minutes early, I sat there. Before family arrived.
In peace, I read recovery literature, given to me when I felt like
carrying on my shoulders suicide. Handed to me by the man
who showered words at my first anonymous meeting — about
hummingbirds & godshots.

As I read, a hummingbird
  descended to greet me.

Hello grandpa,   I said. It
  vanished.

Grandma & others appeared
  from the distance.

Roaming this dusty forest of
  memories.

Words & videos were
  spoken, murmured & hummed.

Narration in
  song...

Yes, I'm leaving. On a jet plane. Don't know
                    when I'll be
                      back again... —

As ashes scattered, our lot departed
on the trunk of
an old, wise
tree—
w/ knowledge,
& the earth...

returned
a hummingbird.

Hello
Grandpa.

First published in *Placeholder Press*. "Archive."
December 31, 2019.

LETTING YOU IN

HI MY FRIEND

I was thinking about a friend I used to do drugs with.
About how I didn't—and still don't—know
if he's alive or dead.

About how I wore the shirt he gave me
the day I took a
coin commemorating one year of sobriety.

All of this going through my head. . .
fingering the coin in my right-pant-upper pocket. . .
while I walked to the car.

The door half-ajar,
I received a text from a sober friend.
It read,

And bask in the Love Light of God. . .

All of a sudden,
I was hit by an insatiable urge
to write these words before closing the rest of the door. . .

Hi my friend. Thanks for the reminder again.
I don't know where you are,
but I hope where you are
things are going along . . .
Free from the guilt,
Free from the pain,
Hope you no longer wear that quilt of same.
Disregard your boulders -- mental shackles
grow horror -- and
Bask in the Love Light of God.

—I paused for just a few seconds. . . overwhelmed
with emotion. . .

11

And I realized these words penetrating my mind
were no longer just about my friend.
Their scope far wider than a mere therapeutic channel
by which to traverse the vast ocean of feeling flooding me.

No, they expanded into an entirely new realm:
about the anguish of identity and introspection.
Words returned—

So shine on,
Shine on,
Shimmer odd that resourceful bog.
Time to take a dive -- it's not even four
feet high --
into the sea of grateful grace:
Shown along, the river bedrock,

Is reflection that reminds us
of the omen to which we bind lust
to the mind whose make is that of madness,
a profession borne out of sadness,
but the cause we all to break,
too late to re-syndicate

You see that man in the clouds he is you and
I'm found
But you know what dies
Out loud

Shown in the space who we thought we were—
Right now!
The times, the places, the memories—really, all
a blur!

If I could glue my life to pieces, who would I
see
This is not me. This is not you. --
    it does not listen --
What glistens transitions into an omission of
styme.
If you could imagine me, I would tear you apart...

GRATITUDE AFTER BREAKFAST

I USED   to think that meditation was a hoax,
that enlightenment was for those interred in the ground.

I USED   to think it was impossible to cease thinking for more than five seconds.
I secretly believed I knew everything.

I USED   to deem gratitude an unnecessary word.
I hated to stretch my cheekbones into a smile.

I was convinced everyone was a phony.
I USED   to think I was the shit.

I USED   to think I was a piece of shit.
I would be paralyzed by fear for hours.

I would argue with mirrors, threatening to pound my fists into the clear.
I USED   to curse the reflection I feared.

I USED   to stay up all night, dancing in sorrow
without consent, my entire body convulsing.

I watched the sun rising sadness and despaired like a mourner.
Outside rising, inside dying.

I USED   to not know if I was lying or telling the truth.
I spent hours wrestling with my god—myself.

I wake up in the morning, and I say the sh'ma.
Then I make my bed; wash my hands.

I wake up in the morning, and I walk to the room next door.
Then I sit in a chair; listen for an hour.

I wake up in the morning, and sometimes I feel light as a feather.
Then I make breakfast; smile as I wash my bowl.

I wake up in the morning, and I smile at the man in the mirror.

Then I take a shower; hug my soul.

I wake up in the morning, and I thank God.
I know I'm not Him.

Photograph by Joshua Corwin. Italy. 2009
First appeared in *Spectrum Publishing*, "Spectrum Cento - Special Issue."
Pasadena, CA. October 26, 2019.

i dream i sleep lightly

i slide
out
of bed

arms raised,
legs
crossed

i can't re-
call
the cross street
where

my spine

i darted
long before
i ran to
grasp

her face
locked up
like car doors

she drove
into
evaporation

alarm
clock
automatic
locks

my legs
from shivering
out of bed

keys
my spine
like
bars of iron
smelted
into nails:

car keys shapeshifting
silhouette outlines
a dream
splintered

over past blocks
street signs
passed over

she drove
the key-shaped
dream

through
&
threw me

into
evaporation
…

but
i still
dream

i sleep
lightly,
like droplets

candle
wax
drooping
faraway

sweet
brushstrokes

sliding

down

tele-
phone
pole

extinguished
flames
recoiled

waxing

illumination

I PUT ON THE SUIT

I put on the suit,
tie the façade –
knot a lie. I'm
just buttoning up
the barrier
between you and
the real me.

I put on the suit,
tie the façade –
knot a lie. . .
button barrier. . .
Dressy slip-ons
to insist you
look this way.

I put on the suit,
tie the façade –
knot a lie. . .
button barrier. . .
dressy slip-ons. . .
Belt pain
to suck it in,
—stomaching
letting it all out.

I put on the suit,
tie the façade –
knot a lie. . .
button barrier. . .
dressy slip-ons. . .
belt pain. . .
Long, black socks
so I can't feel
my own skin
—don't know
that I'm lying
to myself. . .
. . .so that I can
do the trick—
sell the pitch:
who you want
me to be.

I put on the suit,
tie the façade –
knot a lie. . .
button barrier. . .
dressy slip-ons. . .
belt pain. . .
long, black socks. . .
Shiny wristwatch
to cover up the
scars where I slit
my authenticity.

The watch is too
tight. This, too,
is purposeful.
It holds down
the pulse
of the real me.

Artwork by Joshua Corwin – "faces" 2019

THE UPDATE

I tread transgressions
against how far I've come
as a kid diagnosed
on the autism spectrum

at the age of 5
and processing delay
at 6
along with anxiety disorder
and ADHD —

I don't want to repeat
circles, with my feet.
One smaller and the other
— reminds me of my mind.

Neurotypical.

       [also, alcoholic —
               Thank God I'm sober,
               but that's
      another story.]

Like a pacifist in rage
I need to accept my brain chemistry.
But persevere.
Circles.

Those feet
make them.
Quake.

And color loses its vivacity…

Like the squeamish self I am—

(Just
see me at the doctor.

Please.
Don't.
I'm embarrassed,
by how I fade.)

O, it's so hard
to fit in
when you're hardwired
to differ.

Range
like a spectrum of shapes:

I circle,
but I transcend.
But because I do,
I have these fits

{usually every 3 months or so,
sometimes once a year}

It comes from acting
  typical
    when you're
        atypical.

— did I tell you I had to learn
  thousands of idioms?
             [I thought ...
               when someone
               said, "it's raining
               cats and dogs,"
          That it was.]
— flashcards of rules...

I don't want to rock back and forth,
    as I pass on going out the door,
        because I am now the floor…
    unable to speak
  when I have so much to say…

That happens every now and then…
    and my feet repeat themselves in circles…

around a shape – a square or rectangle or circle perfect:
  the kitchen table, where Dad is late
  because he's paying the bills,
  so I can get the therapy I need,
  and the speech therapy
  — to learn idioms … like … "it's raining cats and dogs"
  — *I feel like* "it's raining cats and dogs:"
the words and screams of atypicality,
in dysfunctional
familiac ways – words invented

I have so much to hear.
I have so much to say.

I'm trying to not repeat the circle and fall on the ground…

But perhaps. Putting on the guise
and persevering like I do.

Perhaps, I need to fall.
  Perhaps, I need to circle.

How else could I draw the line
of when it's time to stop the update?

First published in *Placeholder Press*. "Archive."
December 31, 2019.

JOSHUA CORWIN

JOSHUA CORWIN

Photograph by Lori Carr. Pacific Palisades. 1997/98

55,555

A wall washer.
Squishing spiders.
Mom's job – I told my teacher in Kindergarten.

A fuckup – Dad yelling at me.
Running
In pajamas, holding toothbrush, 2 miles on Sunset.

A calculator-----------------
$$55,555$$
$$55,555$$
$$55,555$$
$$55,555$$
$$\text{x } 55,555$$

Waiting – 2nd-grade hands want write answers to
repeating patterns
Stuck in 405 traffic with Mom

A child starting to cry.
Tears
I remember

A movie a week to forget.
Emotional escape
To remember to forget

Hell – growing up feeling misunderstood $55,555^5$ times.
A slice of paradise where Mom likes to vacation – 1st-grade
answer to teacher's question, "What is an island?"

I have autism – Kindergarten teacher inspires Mom to wash walls.

The thing is
Spider's blood stains
like mental cobwebs,
Runs deeper than time stuck on the 405 freeway,
Puzzles a 2nd grader more than repeating patterns.
More than an adult child
Still running to islands, but returning to the 405.
Puzzled- he starts to cry

Tears,
Calculating his own value.
After remembering what it feels like
to be misunderstood
more than 55,555 x 55,555 x 55,555 x 55,555 x 55,555 times.

MEMORY SMILE

I see homeless
in the Santa Monica street.

I'm in Starbucks
Out a window… a memory

A colleague I tried to help get sober

My age (between 24 and 26)

White Jewish male,
upper middle-class,
and an only child, like me.

ASD, ADHD,
Anxiety Disorder,
Processing Delay, like me.

Marijuana addict, like me.

He stayed sober
sheer self-will.

Refused help.

His mind wouldn't let him.
He couldn't say the words.
When he tried to vocalize them,
his mind fought back.

The space of death can be a human being.

A cloak distracting miscellaneous illnesses—
mental health specialists couldn't help him,
his mind shielded him

—wouldn't even let
him have knowledge of
his

Helplessness,
inability to ask—
becoming positive that you'd rather
be insincere & incinerated—

creating
a space
of death
...

I peer through the window

    I.   He convinced himself homeless
    II.   Peer through a memory:
    III. ASD, ADHD, Anxiety.
           Processing. Delay—
    IV. Friends only colleagues.
    V.   I'm too busy,
           out the window of compassion:
    VI. Am I a memory?
    VII. A garbage bin, the eyes
           reflection
    VIII. himself, shot meth, OD on fentanyl.
    IX. He said he'd never be homeless.
    X.   He'd never do meth.
    XI. Only smoke weed.
    X.   Maybe drink every now and then.

I found out he had passed from another friend—
a colleague

Oozing windows ...

I think the memory died.

So why not just smile?

Photograph by Joshua Corwin – "Sunflowers." Italy. 2009

SEPTEMBER 11, 2018 – ROSH HASHANAH

I had a panic attack last night with my dad. My inner Shofar was crying. I was on the floor immobilized and lost voluntary movement. And I cursed and disrespected my dad. I gained voluntary control of my body as I talked to my sponsor over the course of an hour. And then I wept and felt his pain and my dad's pain and allowed myself to feel my own... I had skipped breakfast for the last 3 days in a row, had been getting about 5 ½ hrs of sleep a night for the last 4 days, and hadn't listened to Chassidic lectures for the last 2 days.

My neshamah was weakening.

I needed a reminder of God's love, and to remember to be grateful for where I have come as a person with significant autism and learning disabilities, so much so that my mom and dad were skeptical that I would ever be able to get a bar mitzvah or go to college.

I am now 3 years sober by the grace of God. I am in my senior year at Pitzer. I was asked last week by the Chabad rabbi in Claremont to lead the shofar today. I have a dinner date with a girl who is in two of my classes, Psychology of Mindfulness and Science of Life-Changing Events.

Can I apply the knowledge from these classes to my life? And also be mindful of my own psychology and grateful for the events that have changed life? Can I be mindful of the science that God is with me here right now?

Can I blow the shofar of love and empathy? And carry it on for this moment and the next?

First published in *The Art of Autism*. January 24, 2020.

REVELATION

EYES WIDE OPEN

What is the perfect day but today?
What is the perfect moment but now?

What more could you ask for?
What more could you ask for?

Haven't you seen the divinity lines?
Haven't you witnessed the spaciousness of all-mind?

Haven't you had enough?
Haven't you had enough?

Clay sculptures decreed sieges
Across time - across space

The all-time lay awake, *lay awake*
Golden scepter, golden mace

Zeus cried on Mount Olympus
Hades shouted, "Forsake!"

When name and notion are delimited
not but combined into a single unit:

a sign is downcast.
Gone to waste. *Gone to waste.*

Like Euripides in Kingdom Come
Like the Clementine Assassin,

Lady Truth laid her loose
As Fortune and Fame

She - the double day lauded over
the keys to the thronic enclave

Slated behind the signs
Restless are no-minds

But ye have little faith
Allotted - have yet no time to waste

For rhyme or reason
I give thee the treason
For whom the bell tolls

Fortune favors those souls
who never doth grow old

And grovel to the master,
as dawn meets the day

And eyes wide open
Awaken in the night

Lay to waste, *lay to waste*

I CAN SEE THE WRITING ON THE WALL

What is life but a dream of the dying sun?
What is mine but a trip of the forgotten Son?
What is time but a message from all ages?
What is love but you and I?
Counterparts and renegades and
What is mine and what is yours? — a fluke.

(Touch me now.)

My body is but a lemon drop.
Cool that renegade down with some wine.
Ageless are the dying ones.
  Kyrie, eleison!
Heaven help us humankind.
  Kyrie, eleison!

You are a painting in my mind's eye.
Lifeless – you're but a tapestry on the wall;
Enthroned by the shadows that you sent my way,
I can see the writing on the wall.
Oh, I can see the writing on the wall. . .

Sheltered are the lonely who succumbed to this.
Blissful are the chosen immigrants of that god-awful Son.
Like Eucharists, leftovers I found in the kitchen,
Transubstantiated into fucked-up America.

You could train them like circus lions
flutter forward, parsing SEAs of eutrophication
Or you could let them glow free like this note.
Impinging on the strings of impunity,
Without immunity this lovelight won't flow.

Take me on a trip in your retroactive haze.
Irrigate the lotus-algae skulls.
Will I drown deep in this abyssal gorge?
Or satori-Cally effervesce this oceanic ache I mourn?

Bigly consecrate your transubstantiation fuck —
   Hosanna!
Kill the boy I forgot to love!
    Cui prodest!
Like Isaac and Jacob,
You are God's forgotten Sons.

Write me a letter on the wall of your blissed-out state;
Lest I find a lesson hidden on the wall of your mental state.
Conscious are the nonviolent intoxicated brains
Beat me up inside with tears issuing from my eyes,
Beat me up inside and claim my mind with woeful cries.

And crimes against humanity
Are crimes against your ways;
And times I evoke others' potentials,
I feel like a renegade.

When demons come and go,
I can see the writings on the wall fade.
Etchings are replaced by no etchings at all,
Metaphors forgotten
This chimeric glance. . .

Photograph by Joshua Corwin – "La révolution."
Paris, France. 2011

ĀNANDA

I was never born
Therefore I cannot die

I was grown —
like a lotus blossoms —
In-and-out of sangha
across ten-thousand kalpas

They say, I was born
in this form
on the day the
Buddha attained It

But my form is never complete -
like a process without a pattern -
So I never began
So I never become
So I never go

I am nothing
and I am everything
I am everyone
and I am no one
No thing points to my essence
My essence is no thing
like a thing - a reified illusion -
a magic trick -
the label that is My Name
Paints It
and Paints all that can be seen,
Experienced or conceived

It is impossible
Not to Feel My Name:
Ānanda

BODHISATTVA IN BUENOS AIRES

Bodhisattva in Buenos Aires
Adieu I bid you
A Precautionary Reminder
Man unhooked her saboteur
A siege to die for
And live back in time or
Try toward
A rising Thor

You're an aging arch
A surmising bark
Wag a tail for me, baby
You're the hail of lightning Thunder Dome is striking
Me crazy
It's so gravy

It's a groovy Tuesday in Baltimore
And I see you
And it's the hallmark card of my dreams

You com-creep me - and it completes me
Just a penny full of wishing wells
Swelling downstream eternity
Loading uphill rolling rivers
In the green murkiness of Rea

Call me crazy
But am I delaying?
My happy happenings
Dust of DeMarcus
Marco Polo found his water polo team

There's something happening somewhere
Awesome worlds whizzing whee

You know it comes and goes somewhere
Somewhere somehow
I'll find another crease from which to breathe
You know what they say
At least Nietzsche said
God is dead
But hey baby
Gaiety is with the geishas
And the antelopes play with the zebras
The Bodhisattva's in Buenos Aires

Photograph by Joshua Corwin. Italy. 2009

I REMEMBER WHEN MOTHER DANCED INTO THE FOREST

I remember when mother danced into the forest. Not physically, but into my eye.
I could hear her calling raindrops. Flying right past the daybreaking crimson tide.
Erroneous thought – though these misforgivings might sound – I can hear them
              Wide   awake.
Won't you   accompany me into   the forest.   Right where Mom
                                      And I
                         embraced.

You are your own mother seeking
                         Solace from the grain.
I've heard their failings   or subtle   miscontrivances
       Trying to usher in the working   w i n d o w s
But if you could ream it into   s p a c e   like expedited forum
      Can't we dream it past the glistening overtures?
      Like a God-given pointillist,
 I know the lilacs   are
    Still in the works?

    Meadows of a quietude overturn the spaulders of
        Incredible sorrows.
    Ironic housed into the mass of granite like the grain of
    The planet.
        Crying into eyes overbearing like the willows of
Veneer.   I can see your golden slumber start to shine
   Into the nearest larvae:
      Like prowess in the ride.

WHISTLING INTO WIT / STILLNESS SPEAKS TO THE WAITING

whistling into wit   how fun   earworms   take
accomplice   on this   turquoise embroidered   waltz

a pedigree   overtures   no longer   current
   in the seeds' cure   --   can't you   entertain the

i   want   to have   a term at   being for

it

but i can't forget you   the way the sun   sprains
                                        itself past courage.

We aren't   entitled   to   camouflage.   but
              it   is   OK
to embrace   this   train.   We aren't   going
           very far.   Follow   it   into

the   last   pack of   longings.   And it'll
        work   out   as you   never
     knew it   would . . .

just ask the silence.
   stillness speaks to the waiting.

WALKING ON WATERFALLS / THE EARTH IS SOULED

Walking on waterfalls,   I remember

        when mother danced into the forest.

    As if she could --

could call back

      the wind…   Her footsteps echoing,

     'The earth is souled. . .'

        just ask the silence

          stillness speaks to the waiting

     'The earth is souled. . .'   the wind

        whistling into wit.

    As if I could --

could call back

      the wind…   Its footsteps echoing,

     'The earth is souled. . .'

        just ask the silence

          stillness speaks to the waiting

Walking on waterfalls,   it remembers

        when mother danced into the forest.

    But it can –

can call back

      the wind…   It echoes me into footsteps remembering

     'The earth is souled. . .'

42

Photograph by Joshua Corwin. Yellowstone National Park. 2007

I

Reading complexity right,

its poetry does its truth.
Does it truly matter?
yes, it does to me.

if I only knew—
who am I?

DON'T

I liked its sound   so I looked up

the definition of ownership.

Noun. the act, state, or right of possessing

something   I didn't understand   so I looked up

the definition of   possession

to find out   what I owned.

Photograph by Joshua Corwin. Santa Monica City College. 2016

12:01 AM

I can hear the shine in your eyes
on the other end of the telephone.

When I speak like this,
I feel authentic
and not heavy.

I don't have to tattoo meaning in the air
to know what you mean.

I remember when you first told me…
apropos of nothing…
about the different levels of charitable donation.

I was sitting right across from you — over there.
(You in that armchair, me in this one: our eyes.)

You said there's the donor who gives large sums
and puts a placard on the wall, signifying
who it's from;

and then there's the other one who gives…
but remains anonymous.

Your words hanging like a phantom,
I didn't have to be who I thought I was;

you were once me,
once where I was…

In that moment, I knew.

First published in *Al-Khemia Poetica*. September 3, 2019.

I AM NOT ME

I   silently   expand   noise

that   is   not   silent

I   noisily   contract silence

that   is   not   noise

All form
  never sees
All ways
  never been
All lies
  never witnessed

I   a m   n o t   M e.

I RECALL THE RITUAL

I would pray for ambulances, exhale white light to drivers,
shut eyes and imagine what they might be feeling.
Translucent, a silhouette ghost, I'd wrap myself around them,
hug their inner child until they remembered courage.

Visualizing what it might look like for the driver in motion,
scenes darting past eyes, hoping to get there in time,
praying for safe arrival.

Hands clasp heart, grip vehicles to roadsides.

Eyes glistening compassion.

I'd ask their families, friends, loved ones
be comforted and guided.

I would then be reminded by these words:

God, thank You for my life, for everything and for everyone,
for all that You have given and all that You have taken away.
What can I do for You, God? How can I be helpful to You and my fellows?
Would You please direct my thinking, guide my words?

All this took a minute or two.
If not less…

Washing dishes in the sink, I recall the ritual.

It's been a while…

But that I recall the ritual
is enough to start changing,
and doing what I believe in.

Perhaps you have a ritual?

MAYBE SOMETIMES

Maybe sometimes
I get
to just
breathe

...but
  there's such a
  resistance
  to such
  simple problems

But... usually...
I just deter
Them incongruent
To my destiny-faded
Repentance

LIFE

I glide / I slide / I criss-cross time
I renovate your looking-glass eyes

In heaven / there is no find
Pale / wail / I see you moan
The meaning is gonna get you stoned

A thousand paper folds
For a thousand paper cuts
Cute like napkin, wipe away the smut

Floating
          - blowing -
Breaths of eels
Electric lights
— vexation: fright (into the blues, under oceanic suns)
— nine times ten is nine times longer than what I need
81 years — a dream

Photograph by Joshua Corwin. Downtown Los Angeles. 2016

EMBRACE ME

I/You feel like doing art naked stroking God/me with paintbrushes
and/or with knives;

I feel like leafing through memories with Your/my eyes stealing kisses
with immanence and/or with transcendence;

I/You feel like embracing You/me in garments draped with needles,
with cloves and/or with thyme;

I/You feel like singing songs of somber and solace. But
they (knives who like to whisper like ships which like to bristle on rocky waters)

call it solitude:
a split personality of isolation (lick me/You into my/Your meditation. . .)

I/You feel like kicking off/on the garments draped with needles,
with cloves and/or with thyme;

drop-dead gorgeousness.
as they (the knives who whisper like ships which like to bristle on rocky waters)

poke fun and toy with me; they like to
spin me around like flying saucers

(embrace me. . .)

I'm all alien to y'all;
I'm already broken into my mind   (like a pair of New Balance shoes)

— you know, a kind that smoked itself like bacon
and burst into flames lavishing electric lights.

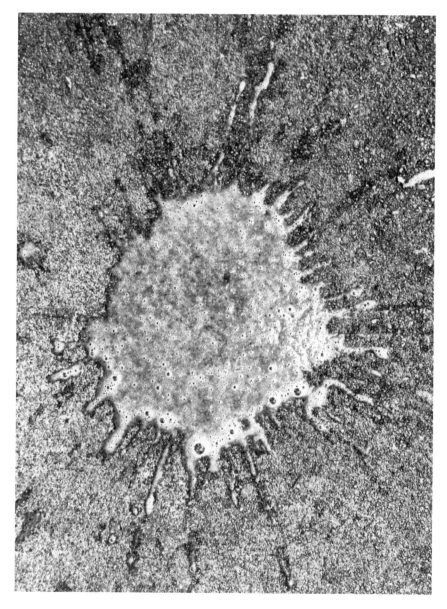

Photograph by Joshua Corwin – "Spilled Milk." Pasadena. 2019

STILL FORSAKEN

There are others like us.
We're like x-people of creativity.
I've met them;
and you have too—
stop… forgetting.

Enact the sovereign state
of temporal qualia.
Without misperception;
strike your head like the gladiator—
the original one… before Rumi.

Cripple your soul into infinity
so waters feel your drops,
like loose eyelashes;
strewn into the wind—
of plenty… yet still forsaken.

First published in *Ginosko Literary Journal*, Issue 24.

Artwork and Photograph by Joshua Corwin – "Brushes" 2019

UNTITLED FEELINGS

Sometimes, I just want to cry
and hide away from the rest
of the world.

You see, this voice ringing,
screaming in my head — tells
me lies. I know they aren't
grounded in reality, but sometimes
I take flight from reality,
stare at this mirror & cry.
I don't know who I'm looking at.

But there are other times
when the mirror is golden beauty
reflects joyous heaven.

BUT I DON'T SEE

I cry tears
  breathe reason
die faith
  walk this body
born myself.

I write hands
  words listen
thoughts hear
  But I   don't   see.

APOPHATIC TRADITION

Truth transpires like ire.
You never catch a glance.

All that is visible,
you never know

without your coat
of armor glistening
                    in
                          the
                                water.

THE GATE IS NOT A GATE

Until it speaks,
Until you don't say,
Your mind is shut.

The gate is not a gate.

First published in *Ginosko Literary Journal*, Issue 24.

MAY YOU FIND JOY

Wishing you the most extravagant day filled with adventure and content!

I wish you security in the face of adversity, and uncertainty
while wearing a loose cloak of serenity.

I hope you don't know what happens today. I hope you never find out.
I hope you live each moment as though there is no next—and as though
the concept of "now" is foreign.

I hope you never understand the concept of "now," that way
you'll always live it.

I hope you never realize that you're living it—that way
you'll always be free.

Wishing you the most extravagant day filled with adventure and content!

ACKNOWLEDGMENTS

I would like to thank Brenda Petrakos of Baxter Daniels Ink Press/International Word Bank for publishing this collection. I would also like to thank Coco "Corrine Marie Rodriguez," my dear editor and friend, for endless hours of late-night editing. I would also like to thank editor-in-chief of *Spectrum Publishing*, Don "Kingfisher" Campbell, as well G. T. Foster, for publishing my first poem and more. I would like to express thanks to Marie C. Lecrivain for publishing me in *Al-Khemia Poetica, poeticdiversity* and for nominating my poem "12:01 AM" for the 2019 Pushcart Prize.

Special thanks to my dear friend Alan Bail for his emotional support and encouragement; as well as to my mother, Susan, for her careful reading of a version of the manuscript. I would like to thank my father, Scott, for his legal counsel and reading the manuscript. Thank you to Rich Lenke for his invaluable help in laying out the front and back cover.

I would like to thank Albert Wachtel for his incredible words in the foreword to *Becoming Vulnerable*. (While perusing Scott Hall in Pitzer College the week before graduation, Al suggested I submit some of my poetry for publication. If it weren't for him, it is very likely I would not have taken it upon myself to write this book.)

Additional thanks to Mike Sonksen (who also put me in contact with Don), Ellyn Maybe, David Rocklin, Elaine Hall, Rich Ferguson, Barbara Straus Lodge and Barry Prizant for their words and insight on *Becoming Vulnerable*. Also thank you to Elena Karina Byrne, Richard Modiano, Nelson Gary, Lida Parent-Harris, S.A. Griffin, Michael C. Ford and Jonathan K. Rice.

Last, and most important, I would like to acknowledge my dear late grandfather, Mert Freeman, for his love and support—not only during his lifetime, but also after his departure—inspiring me to 'get my work out there' and write a collection of poetry.

ABOUT THE AUTHOR

Los Angeles native **Joshua Corwin** is a neurodiverse poet with a B.A. in mathematics and a minor in philosophy from Pitzer College ('19). Nominated for the 2019 Pushcart Prize, his work is published in *Al-Khemia Poetica, Spectrum Publishing, The Art of Autism, Placeholder Press, The Ephimiliar Journal, Ginosko Literary Journal* and *poeticdiversity*. His debut poetry collection, *Becoming Vulnerable*, details his experience with autism, addiction, sobriety and spirituality (Baxter Daniels Ink Press/International Word Bank; April 2020). Corwin hosts the poetry podcast "Assiduous Dust." Bringing to The Miracle Project, an autism nonprofit, poetry classes for individuals of all abilities, including those with autism recovering from addiction (starting April 2020). He writes to honor his grandpa, Mert, whose last words to him were "Don't ever stop writing."